Spread the Love

The PB & J Cookbook

BY: Valeria Ray

License Notes

Copyright © 2019 Valeria Ray All Rights Reserved

All rights to the content of this book are reserved by the Author without exception unless permission is given stating otherwise.

The Author have no claims as to the authenticity of the content and the Reader bears all responsibility and risk when following the content. The Author is not liable for any reparations, damages, accidents, injuries or other incidents occurring from the Reader following all or part of this publication.

A Special Reward for Purchasing My Book!

Thank you, cherished reader, for purchasing my book and taking the time to read it. As a special reward for your decision, I would like to offer a gift of free and discounted books directly to your inbox. All you need to do is fill in the box below with your email address and name to start getting amazing offers in the comfort of your own home. You will never miss an offer because a reminder will be sent to you. Never miss a deal and get great deals without having to leave the house! Subscribe now and start saving!

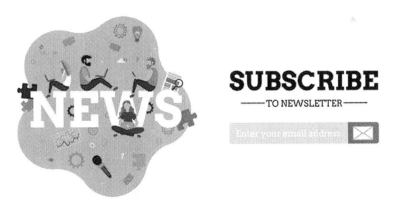

https://valeria-ray.gr8.com

Contents

Delicious Peanut Butter Recipes

MMMMMMMMMMMMMMMMMMMMMMMMMMMMMMMMMMMM

Chapter I - Sweet Treats

MMMMMMMMMMMMMMMMMMMMMMMMMMMMMMMMMM

(1) Peanut Butter & Jelly Fudge

Scrummy little bites of sweet, jammy fudge!

Makes: 64

Cooking Time: 8hours 15mins

List of Ingredients:

- 1 (7½ ounce) jar marshmallow cream
- 1 (11 ounce) package white chocolate chips
- ¾ cup smooth peanut butter
- ¼ cup crunchy peanut butter
- ¾ cup unsalted butter
- 2 ½ cups granulated sugar
- Pinch sea salt
- 1 cup heavy whipping cream
- ¾ cup strawberry jam

MMMMMMMMMMMMMMMMMMMMMMMMMMMMMMMMMM

Methods:

1. Using parchment paper, line an 8" square baking dish and set to one side.

2. In a mixing bowl, combine the marshmallow cream with the white chocolate chips, smooth peanut butter, and crunchy peanut butter. Set to one side.

3. In a pan, combine the unsalted butter together with the sugar, salt and whipping cream and over moderate to high heat boil for 4 minutes.

4. Pour the boiling butter mixture over the marshmallow cream mixture and using an electric mixer, beat until smooth and creamy, this will take between 1-2 minutes.

5. Pour approximately half of the mixture into the bottom of the baking dish. Top with the strawberry jam and using a blunt kitchen knife, swirl the jam into the fudge. Top the remaining fudge mixture. Once again, swirl to combine the jam with the peanut butter.

6. Transfer to the fridge, overnight.

7. Cut into 64 bite-sized pieces and enjoy.

8. Store any leftover fudge in an airtight container in the fridge for up to 14 days.

(2) Italian-Style Tiramisu with PB&J

Peanut butter and jelly add an American twist on a favorite Italian dessert.

Makes: 8-10

Cooking Time: 8hours 20mins

List of Ingredients:

- ½ cup smooth peanut butter
- 8 ounces cream cheese (room temperature)
- 1¼ cups powdered sugar
- 1 teaspoon vanilla essence
- 1 cup heavy cream (divided)
- ½ cup seedless raspberry jam
- ⅓ cup water
- 16 Italian-style crisp finger sponge biscuits
- 4 cups fresh raspberries
- Chocolate shavings (to garnish)
- Powdered sugar (to serve)

MMMMMMMMMMMMMMMMMMMMMMMMMMMMMMMMMMMMM

Methods:

1. In a bowl, combine and beat the peanut butter with the cream cheese, powdered sugar, vanilla essence and ½ cup of cream, for 3-4 minutes, until light and fluffy. Add the remaining cream and beat for 2 minutes, until smooth. Take care not to overbeat.

2. In a small bowl, whisk the raspberry jam with the water until combined.

3. Spoon approximately 3 tablespoons of the raspberry jam mixture into a 9x5" loaf tin. Cover the jam with 8 of the sponge fingers, arranging them in a single layer, lengthwise. Brush the finger sponge biscuits with the remaining jam. You may appear to have excess liquid, but this is not a problem as it will absorb.

4. Spread half of the peanut butter mixture over the sponge fingers and top with 2 cups of fresh raspberries. Arrange the remaining 8 sponge fingers on top of the raspberries, lengthwise.

5. Brush the fingers with the remaining jam and spread with the remaining peanut mixture.

6. Cover with kitchen wrap and transfer to the fridge, overnight.

7. When you are ready to serve, uncover, and scatter with the remaining fresh raspberries and chocolate shavings.

8. Dust with powdered sugar.

(3) Chocolate Dipped Bacon Burger with PB&J

Forget the cheese and ketchup; these sweet and savory patties are a mouth-watering alternative.

Makes: 4

Cooking Time: 1hour 5mins

List of Ingredients:

- 8 strips uncooked bacon
- ½ cup semi-sweet chocolate chips
- ½ cup butter
- 2 pounds ground beef
- 1 teaspoon salt
- 1½ teaspoons black pepper
- 1 medium egg
- 8 fresh waffles
- ½ cup smooth peanut butter
- ½ cup strawberry jam

MMMMMMMMMMMMMMMMMMMMMMMMMMMMMMMMMMMM

Methods:

1. Preheat the main oven to 350 degrees F.

2. Arrange the bacon on a baking sheet, lined with parchment paper and cook until crispy; this will take around 12 minutes.

3. Pat the bacon with kitchen paper and put to one side to cool to around room temperature.

4. Fill a pot to the halfway mark with water and bring to a gentle boil.

5. Add the chocolate chips to a stainless steel bowl and set it over the pot of boiling water, while making sure that the bottom of the bowl does not come into contact with the water.

6. Add the butter to a microwave-safe bowl and in 20-second interval, microwave until melted.

7. Add the butter to the chocolate and whisk until smooth.

8. Dip the crispy bacon in the melted chocolate and place on the baking sheet.

9. Transfer to the fridge until hardened, this will take between 15-20 minutes.

10. Next, make the patties. In a bowl, combine the ground beef with the salt, pepper, and egg until combined.

11. Evenly divide the mixture into 4 balls and gently press each of the balls between two sheets of parchment paper for make patties approximately ¼ "thick.

12. In a skillet, over moderate to high heat, cook the burgers until the meat is sufficiently cooked through and no longer pink.

13. In the meantime, and while the burgers are cooking, toast the waffles.

14. Spread each waffle with 2 tablespoons each of peanut butter and jam.

15. Top each burger with 2 slices of chocolate coated bacon and sandwich between two toasted waffles.

(4) Banana Flautas with PB&J

A quick and tasty treat that makes a yummy breakfast or afternoon pick-me-up.

Makes: 2

Cooking Time: 5mins

List of Ingredients:

- 2 flour tortillas
- 4 tablespoons smooth peanut butter
- 2 tablespoons raspberry jelly
- 2 ripe, medium bananas (peeled)

MMMMMMMMMMMMMMMMMMMMMMMMMMMMMMMMMMMMMM

Methods:

1. Warm the tortillas in the microwave for 10-12 seconds.

2. Spread one side of each tortilla with 2 tablespoons smooth peanut butter.

3. Spread 1 tablespoon raspberry jelly on top.

4. Arrange 1 whole banana at the edge of each tortilla and roll up like a cigar.

5. Enjoy!

(5) Sticky Peanut Butter and Jelly Chicken Wings

A finger-licking good party snack. Your guests will love the way the hot sauce is balanced by the sweet flavors of peanut butter and grape jelly.

Makes: 4-5

Cooking Time: 9hours 10mins

List of Ingredients:

- 1 (10 ounce) jar grape jelly
- ½ cup smooth peanut butter
- ¼ cup red wine vinegar
- ½ teaspoons hot pepper sauce
- ½ teaspoons salt
- 20 chicken drumettes
- Cilantro (chopped, to garnish)

MMMMMMMMMMMMMMMMMMMMMMMMMMMMMMMMMMMMMM

Methods:

1. In a mixing bowl, combine the jelly with the peanut butter, wine vinegar, hot sauce, and salt. Set ½ cup of the marinade to one side.

2. Add the drumettes to the marinade and transfer to the refrigerator, overnight.

3. Arrange the marinated drumettes on a greased oven rack placed inside an aluminum foil-lined baking tray and bake in the oven at 375 degrees F for half an hour.

4. Remove the drumettes from the oven and flip each one over. Baste with the sauce in the tray. Continue baking for 20 minutes.

5. Once the chicken is sufficiently cooked and its juices run clear, baste it in the ½ cup of marinade set aside the previous day.

6. Arrange the chicken on a bed of chopped cilantro and serve.

(6) Berry, Butter Bundt Cake

A peanut butter glazed bundt cake is going to make you very popular with friends and neighbors!

Makes: 10-12

Cooking Time: 1hour 25mins

List of Ingredients:

- Butter (to grease)
- 1¾ cups flour
- ¾ teaspoons baking powder
- ¼ teaspoons bicarbonate of soda
- ½ teaspoons salt
- 1¼ cups packed light brown sugar
- ½ cup creamy peanut butter
- 8 tablespoons unsalted butter (room temperature)
- 3 large, organic eggs
- ½ teaspoons vanilla essence
- ⅓ cup whole milk
- ½ cup grape or raspberry jelly

For the glaze:

- 4 tablespoons unsalted butter (melted)
- 3 tablespoons creamy peanut butter
- 2 tablespoons powdered sugar

MMMMMMMMMMMMMMMMMMMMMMMMMMMMMMMMMMMMM

Methods:

1. Preheat the main oven to 360 degrees F. Lightly grease a Bundt (10-cup) pan.

2. In a large bowl, sift in the flour along with the baking powder, bicarb and salt.

3. Beat in the sugar followed by the peanut butter and unsalted butter, using an electric stand mixer on a moderate to high speed, mix for 4-5 minutes, until light and fluffy. Scrape down the sides of the mixing bowl.

4. One at a time, add the eggs, beating well between additions. Continue to beat for a couple of minutes, until the mixture is light and creamy.

5. Reduce the mixer speed to moderate to low and beat in the vanilla essence, followed by the flour-salt mixture in 3 additions. Add the milk in 2 additions. You must begin and end with the flour, beating until just blended.

6. Pour approximately half of the batter into the pan.

7. Spoon the jelly into the middle of the batter. Spoon the remaining batter on top and smooth out until even.

8. Bake in the oven, on the middle rack, until springy to the touch, and allow to rest in the pan for 3-4 minutes, before turning out onto a wire baking rack.

9. To make the glaze. In a bowl, beat the butter with the peanut butter and powdered sugar until silky. Spoon the glaze over the cake and evenly spread.

10. Slice and serve.

(7) Smokin' Hot Peanut Butter and Jelly Ribs

Smoking adds flavor to an already awesome recipe. Invite a few friends around for a cook-out and enjoy these mouth-watering ribs.

Makes: 4-6

Cooking Time: 3hours 45mins

List of Ingredients:

Rub:

- 2 tablespoons prepared chili powder
- 2 tablespoons paprika
- 2 tablespoons packed light brown sugar
- 1 tablespoon onion granules
- 1 tablespoon sea salt
- 1 tablespoon milled black pepper

For the ribs:

- 4 (3 pound) racks of baby back ribs

Glaze:

- 1 cup raspberry preserves
- ½ cup unsweetened fresh apple juice
- 2 tablespoons balsamic vinegar

For the sauce:

- 1 cup smooth peanut butter
- ¾-1 cup unsweetened fresh apple juice (divided)
- 2 tablespoons apple cider

MMMMMMMMMMMMMMMMMMMMMMMMMMMMMMMMMMMM

Methods:

1. In a bowl combine the rub ingredients; the chili powder, paprika, brown sugar, onion granules, sea salt and black pepper.

2. Using a blunt kitchen knife, lift and pull off each membrane of the baby back ribs. You do this by sliding the tip of the knife under the membrane in the center of the back of each rack.

3. Season the racks with the rub making sure that the meaty side of each rack is generously coated. Set the racks to one side at room temperature while you prepare your smoker.

4. Prepare your smoker for low heat of between 250-300 degrees, while filling the water pan approximately ¾ full with water.

5. Add the chunks of wood to the charcoal and securely close the lid.

6. As soon as you see smoke, arrange the racks, bone side facing down, over indirect and very low heat. Secure the lid and close the top vent to no more than halfway.

7. Cook the ribs at 250-300 degrees for 2 ½ hours.

8. In the meantime, prepare the glaze.

9. To make the glaze, add the raspberry preserves, apple juice, and balsamic vinegar to a pan and over moderate heat simmer for 3-5 minutes, while occasionally stirring. Remove the pan from the heat.

10. Next, make the sauce. In a second pan, combine the peanut butter with ½ cup of fresh apple juice followed by the vinegar. Over moderate heat, cook slowly for 2 minutes, until the sauce is smooth. You will need to whisk the sauce continually. Remove the pan from the heat.

11. When 2 ½ hours of cooking time for the ribs has elapsed, lightly brush each rack on both sides with the glaze and continue to cook for half an hour.

12. After a total of 3 hours cooking, the ribs will have receded from the bone by approximately ¼ ". If this is not the case, continue to cook until they do.

13. They are sufficiently cooed when the middle of the rack bends and the meat easily comes away from the bone.

14. Return the pan with the peanut sauce to the stove over moderate heat.

15. Add between ¼ -1/2 cup of the remaining juice and warm for 2-3 minutes, while occasionally stirring.

16. Lightly brush each rack with additional glaze before cutting into ribs.

17. Serve with peanut sauce and enjoy.

(8) Cheesecake Dessert Dip

Grab some crackers and fruit, and dip into this sinfully sweet peanut butter and jelly cheesecake creation, sprinkled with whole crunchy nuts.

Makes: 8

Cooking Time: 5mins

List of Ingredients:

- 8 ounces full-fat cream cheese (at room temperature)
- 1 cup smooth organic peanut butter
- 2 tablespoons organic honey
- ½ cup strawberry jam
- ¼ cup roasted unsalted peanuts (chopped)

MMMMMMMMMMMMMMMMMMMMMMMMMMMMMMMMMMMM

Methods:

1. Whip up the cream cheese using an electric whisk until fluffy.

2. Whisk in the peanut butter until combined, followed by the honey and jam.

3. Spoon into a serving dish and sprinkle with roasted peanuts.

4. Enjoy straight away with fresh fruit and crackers (or keep chilled until ready to serve).

(9) Roast Pork Loin Stuffed with Peanut Butter and Strawberry Jam

A new and exciting way to serve pork loin which tastes as good as it looks and sounds.

Makes: 6

Cooking Time: 1hour 25mins

List of Ingredients:

- 2 pounds pork loin
- Crunchy peanut butter
- Strawberry or cherry jelly jam
- 1 tablespoon kosher salt
- 1 tablespoon freshly ground black pepper
- 3-4 tablespoons olive oil (for roasting)

MMMMMMMMMMMMMMMMMMMMMMMMMMMMMMMMMMMMMM

Methods:

1. Preheat the main oven to 360 degrees F.

2. Cut the pork loin, on a cutting board, into a long, flat strip. Alternatively, ask your butcher to do this for you.

3. Spread the peanut butter over the whole pork loin. Aim for an even layer that is neither too thick nor too thin.

4. Spread a medium to thick layer of jam over the peanut butter. The jam will help the meat to remain moist.

5. Cut 4 pieces of kitchen string into pieces of around 8-12" long, depending on the size of your pork loin. Lay the pieces of string on a clean worktop approximately 1" apart and parallel to one another.

6. Lay the pork loin, spread side facing upwards on top of the string while making sure that the ends of the string are visible on both sides.

7. Roll the pork up, tie the string, and pull tightly. Some filling will ooze out but this isn't a problem.

8. Next, season the pork by rubbing it with kosher salt and black pepper.

9. Heat 1-2 tablespoons of olive oil in a large frying pan over moderate to high heat.

10. Place the tied up pork in the pan. Don't be concerned if it looks a little messy.

11. Next, seal the meat. Continually turn the meat in the pan to seal it on both sides and ends. Keep doing this until the meat turns from pink to white; this will take around 60 seconds per side.

12. Transfer the pork loin to a roasting tin.

13. Add the remaining oil to the roasting tin, coating the pork loin all over in the oil to prevent it from sticking.

14. Put the pork on the center rack of the preheated oven and cook for 60 minutes, remembering to check every 15 minutes or so that it is not sticking. If it does stick, gently move it slightly.

15. When the pork is sufficiently cooked, transfer it to a cutting board and allow to rest for a few minutes.

16. Slice and serve.

(10) Crunchy Nutty Jam Truffles

These PB&J truffles are a super after-dinner party treat to share with your guests.

Makes: 24

Cooking Time: 20mins

List of Ingredients:

- 2 tablespoons butter
- 1 cup smooth peanut butter
- 2 cups powdered sugar
- 2 tablespoons whole milk
- ½ cup strawberry jam
- 12 ounces dark chocolate (melted)

MMMMMMMMMMMMMMMMMMMMMMMMMMMMMMMMMMMM

Methods:

1. Using either a handheld or stand mixer, combine the butter with the smooth peanut butter, powdered sugar and milk.

2. With parchment paper, line a baking sheet.

3. Using clean hands, form the butter mixture into balls of approximately 1" in diameter.

4. Gently press your finger on top of each ball to make an indent. Fill the indent with jam.

5. Arrange the truffles on the prepared baking sheet and place in the freezer for a minimum of 60 minutes.

6. In the meantime, and using a double boiler, melt the dark chocolate, stirring until smooth.

7. Remove the baking sheet from the freezer and dip each ball into the melted chocolate.

8. Return the chocolate dipped truffles to the baking sheet and place in the freezer until set, for around half an hour.

9. Store in an airtight and re-sealable container in the fridge.

(11) Peanut Butter Noodle Salad

You will be pleasantly surprised just how good this combination of ingredients tastes. You can also serve this noodle salad alongside a grilled chicken breast for a heartier meal.

Makes: 4

Cooking Time: 10mins

List of Ingredients:

- 8 ounces whole grain spaghetti (cooked, drained)
- ½ cup crunchy peanut butter
- ⅓ cup grape jelly
- ¼ cup store-bought Italian dressing
- 1 small cucumber (peeled, seeded, chopped)
- 1 red bell pepper (sliced)
- 1 green onion (thinly sliced)

MMMMMMMMMMMMMMMMMMMMMMMMMMMMMMMMMMMM

Methods:

1. Rinse the cooked noodles with cold water.

2. Add the peanut butter and grape jelly to a microwave safe bowl and microwave in 25-second intervals until melted, whisking until smooth.

3. Add the spaghetti, Italian dressing, cucumber, pepper, and onion to the bowl and stir to combine.

4. Serve either at room temperature or chilled.

(12) Dessert Pizza with Peanut Butter, Jelly & Berries

Pizza doesn't just have to be savory! Tuck into this sweet creation with peanut butter, jelly, and plenty of fresh berries.

Makes: 6

Cooking Time: 25mins

List of Ingredients:

- ¾ cup smooth peanut butter
- 1 readymade (10") pizza crust
- ½ cup grape jelly
- 2 cups fresh berries

MMMMMMMMMMMMMMMMMMMMMMMMMMMMMMMMMMM

Methods:

1. Preheat the main oven to 375 degrees F.

2. In a microwave-safe bowl, warm the peanut butter in a microwave for 20-30 seconds until runny and smooth.

3. Pour the runny peanut butter over the pizza crust and spread out evenly using the back of a spoon.

4. Spread the jam on top of the peanut butter.

5. Arrange the pizza on a baking sheet and pop in the oven for 8-10 minutes.

6. When the topping is gently bubbling remove from the oven and allow to cool a little.

7. Top with fresh berries, slice and enjoy warm.

(13) Peanut Butter and Pineapple Jelly Wood-Grilled Salmon

If you are looking to impress, then look no further than this wood-grilled salmon. It's a real show stopper.

Makes: 3-4

Cooking Time: 25mins

List of Ingredients:

- 3 pounds of fresh skinless, boneless Atlantic salmon
- 1 (24") plant of wood (pre-soaked in water)
- 2 tablespoons sweet and spicy rub
- 3 tablespoons smooth peanut butter (room temperature)
- 3 tablespoons pineapple jelly preserves
- 1 tablespoon water
- 1 cup fresh pineapple (peeled, chopped)
- 2 tablespoons fresh dill (chopped)

MMMMMMMMMMMMMMMMMMMMMMMMMMMMMMMMMMMM

Methods:

1. Preheat your grill to high heat.

2. Lay the salmon, skin side facing downwards on the pre-soaked plank and season with the sweet and spicy rub. Make sure you push the rub into the salmon flesh so that it sticks.

3. Spread the peanut butter all over the surface of the salmon. Use more if necessary to evenly cover.

4. In a small bowl, combine the pineapple preserves with 1 tablespoon of water, stirring to make a thin, spreadable paste. Spread the paste over the peanut butter.

5. Scatter the chopped pineapple and dill over the salmon.

6. Place the plank on the preheated grill and securely close the lid.

7. Bake the salmon on the plank for between 15-20 minutes, until medium done, or until the salmon flakes easily when using a fork. The peanut butter should ideally be soft, and the pineapple jelly preserves slightly caramelized and bubbling.

(14) Fancy French Toast

Don't relegate this breakfast toast to the weekend only. It deserves to be on the menu seven days a week.

Makes: 4

Cooking Time: 5mins

List of Ingredients:

- 1 cup whole milk
- 4 medium eggs
- 2 tablespoons brown sugar
- 1 teaspoon cinnamon
- 1 tablespoon vanilla essence
- 2 cups oatmeal
- 8 slices thick whole grain bread
- ½ cup smooth peanut butter
- ½ cup grape jelly
- Oil and butter (to cook)
- Maple syrup (to drizzle)

MMMMMMMMMMMMMMMMMMMMMMMMMMMMMMMMMM

Methods:

1. Over moderate heat, heat a frying pan or skillet.

2. In a mixing bowl, whisk the milk along with the eggs, brown sugar, cinnamon, and essence.

3. Add the oatmeal to a second mixing bowl.

4. Make 4 peanut butter and jelly sandwiches and dip each sandwich into the wet mixture, followed by the oatmeal, making sure the sandwiches are evenly coated.

5. Add a splash of oil to your skillet along with a dab of butter in the middle of the skillet, doing this will prevent the butter from burning.

6. Slowly cook the sandwiches on both sides until golden; this will take around 3-4 minutes each side.

7. Serve hot, drizzled with maple syrup and enjoy.

(15) PB and Hot J Steak Stir-Fry with Rice

Hot red pepper jelly and creamy smooth peanut butter combine with juicy, tender strips of steak for a weekend treat.

Makes: 4-5

Cooking Time: 20mins

List of Ingredients:

- ⅓ cup of soy sauce
- ⅓ cup of red pepper jelly
- 2 tablespoons smooth peanut butter
- ⅓ cup water
- 2 teaspoons cornstarch
- 3 tablespoons olive oil (divided)
- 1-pound flank steak (thinly sliced)
- 2 cups sugar snap peas
- 3 cups broccoli florets (chopped)
- 1 orange bell pepper (thinly sliced)
- 1 tablespoon garlic (minced)
- 4 green onions (finely chopped)
- 4-5 portions of rice (cooked, hot)

MMMMMMMMMMMMMMMMMMMMMMMMMMMMMMMMMMMM

Methods:

1. Add the soy sauce, red pepper jelly and peanut butter to a mixing bowl.

2. In a second smaller bowl combine the cornstarch with ⅓ cup of water, mixing well to incorporate.

3. Add the cornstarch mixture to the soy sauce-peanut butter mixture.

4. Over high heat, heat 2 tablespoons of oil in a skillet. Add the thinly sliced steak and cook to your preferred level of doneness, around 3-4 minutes. You may need to do this in batches.

5. In a separate skillet or wok, heat the remaining oil. Add the broccoli, peas, bell pepper, garlic and half of the chopped green onions to the pan and cook until fork tender, 2-3 minutes.

6. Add the soy sauce mixture followed by the steak to the wok and while continually stirring, bring to boil. Continue to cook, while occasionally stirring for 60 seconds, or until the sauce has thickened a little.

7. Remove the wok from the heat, add the remaining onions and serve over the hot rice.

(16) Frozen Yogurt Bark with PB&J Swirl

Swap chocolate for yogurt next time you make candy bark. It makes for a yummy sweet treat that is lower in calories and in fat, but just as big on flavor!

Makes: 10-12

Cooking Time: 6 hours 10mins

List of Ingredients:

- 2 cups non-fat vanilla flavor Greek yogurt
- ¼ cup smooth organic peanut butter
- 1 tablespoon organic strawberry jam

MMMMMMMMMMMMMMMMMMMMMMMMMMMMMMMMMMMMMM

Methods:

1. Cover an 8" square baking dish with parchment.

2. Pour the yogurt into the dish and spread into an even layer using a spatula.

3. Warm the peanut butter in the microwave in 10-20 second intervals, until runny. Drizzle the peanut butter over the yogurt and swirl with a cocktail stick.

4. Repeat the same process with the strawberry jam.

5. Freeze the bark for 5-6 hours until solid.

6. Break into shards and enjoy.

(17) Chicken Broth with Peanut Butter and Grape Jelly

A protein rich and tasty broth for those under-the-weather days.

Makes: 4

Cooking Time: 40mins

List of Ingredients:

- 2 tablespoons butter
- 2 tablespoons onion (grated)
- 1 stalk celery (diced)
- 2 tablespoons flour
- 3 cups chicken broth
- ½ cup smooth peanut butter
- Pinch of salt
- 1 cup light cream
- 2 tablespoons roasted peanuts (chopped)
- ½ cup grape jelly

MMMMMMMMMMMMMMMMMMMMMMMMMMMMMMMMMMMM

Methods:

1. Ina saucepan, over low heat, melt the butter.

2. Add the onion followed by the celery and fry for 4-5 minutes.

3. Stir in the flour until combined.

4. Gradually add the chicken broth and allow to simmer for half an hour.

5. Remove the pan from the heat.

6. Strain the broth to remove and discard the vegetables.

7. Stir in the peanut butter, along with the salt and light cream until incorporated.

8. Serve the broth hot and garnish with chopped peanuts and a dollop of grape jelly.

(18) Jelly Popsicles

Your little ones will love these easy-to-make popsicles.

Makes: 4

Cooking Time: 8hours 15mins

List of Ingredients:

- ½ cup smooth peanut butter
- 2 tablespoons honey
- 1 cup whole milk (divided)
- ½ cup raspberry jam

MMMMMMMMMMMMMMMMMMMMMMMMMMMMMMMMMMMM

Methods:

1. In a bowl, combine the peanut butter with the honey, and ½ cup of whole milk, whisking until lump free.

2. In a separate bowl, combine the jam along with the remaining ½ cup of milk and whisk.

3. Pour both mixtures into two separate measuring cups.

4. Add 2 tablespoons of the peanut butter mixture into each popsicle mold. Add 2 tablespoons of the jam mixture to each mold.

5. Transfer the molds to the freezer for half an hour.

6. Remove from the freezer and pour the remaining peanut mixture on top. Place a stick in the center of each cup and return to the freezer for 6-8 hours until solid.

(19) Beef Wraps with PB&J

Wrap and roll! Tasty wraps are an ideal lunch or supper snack, and these are ready from pan to plate in just half an hour.

Makes: 4

Cooking Time: 30mins

List of Ingredients:

- 1-pound ground beef
- ⅓ cup red bell pepper (chopped)
- ½ teaspoons freshly ground black pepper
- ½ cup green onions (chopped)
- 2 ½ tablespoons smooth peanut butter
- 2 tablespoons grape jelly
- 2 tablespoons soy sauce
- 4 medium (8-10") flour tortillas (warm)
- ¼ cup dry roasted peanuts (chopped)

MMMMMMMMMMMMMMMMMMMMMMMMMMMMMMMMMMM

Methods:

1. Over moderate heat, heat a nonstick frying pan.

2. When hot, add the beef along with the pepper, cook until no pink remains, for between 7-10 minutes, using the back of a wooden spoon to break the meat up into crumbles and stirring. Season with pepper.

3. Add the onions, peanut butter, grape jelly and soy sauce and cook, while stirring for a few minutes, until the ingredients are totally combined and the PB&J has melted.

4. Divide the meat mixture between the warm tortillas and garnish with chopped peanuts.

5. Roll and serve.

(20) Jelly S'mores

The classic S'more just got an upgrade with berry jelly and crunchy peanut butter sandwiched together with ooey gooey mallow. Yum!

Makes: 8

Cooking Time: 15mins

List of Ingredients:

- 16 graham cracker squares
- ¼ cup crunchy peanut butter (divided)
- ¼ cup strawberry jelly
- 8 large mallows
- 8 chunks milk chocolate

MMMMMMMMMMMMMMMMMMMMMMMMMMMMMMMMMMMMM

Methods:

1. Spread 8 of the crackers with 2 teaspoons of crunchy peanut butter on one side only and arrange on a cookie sheet lined with aluminum foil.

2. Spread the remaining crackers with 2 teaspoons jelly on one side only and set aside for a moment.

3. Rest a large mallow on top of each of the peanut butter covered crackers. Using a kitchen blowtorch, gently toast the mallows until melting and golden. Place a chocolate chunk on top of each one.

4. Quickly sandwich together with the jelly covered crackers (jelly side facing down) and serve.

(21) Sweet 'n Savory

Bacon, Peanut Butter & Hot Pepper Jelly Sandwich

Take a bacon sandwich to a new level with this amazing combination.

Makes: 1

Cooking Time: 10mins

List of Ingredients:

- 1 whole grain muffin (split in half, lightly toasted)
- 2 tablespoons smooth peanut butter
- 1 tablespoon hot pepper jelly
- 2 slices bacon (cooked)

MMMMMMMMMMMMMMMMMMMMMMMMMMMMMMMMMMMMM

Methods:

1. Spread 1 toasted muffin half with peanut butter.

2. Spread the other half with hot pepper jelly.

3. Sandwich the bacon in between the two and enjoy.

(22) Mini No-Bake PB&J Pies

What could be easier than no-bake pies? Creamy and sweet pies are ideal as an afternoon snack with coffee, tea or soda.

Makes: 12

Cooking Time: 4 hours 35mins

List of Ingredients:

- 3 cups milk (divided)
- ⅓ cup granulated sugar
- ⅛ teaspoons sea salt
- ¼ cup cornstarch
- 3 large egg yolks (lightly beaten)
- ¾ cup creamy, organic peanut butter
- 12 mini graham cracker pie crusts
- ¾ cup grape jelly
- 1 cup heavy cream
- 2 tablespoons powdered sugar
- 2 teaspoons water
- ¼ cup roasted peanuts (coarsely chopped)

MMMMMMMMMMMMMMMMMMMMMMMMMMMMMMMMMMMM

Methods:

1. Over moderate heat, in a large pan, heat 2¾ cups of whole milk until hot. Do not allow to boil.

2. In a mixing bowl, add the sugar with the sea salt and cornstarch, whisking to incorporate.

3. Add the lightly beaten egg yolk and remaining milk, whisking to combine.

4. Add approximately ½ of the heated milk to the egg yolk mixture, whisking until lump free.

5. A little at a time, add the egg mixture to the hot milk and over moderate heat, cook, while continually whisking until the mixture boils and begins to thicken, this will take 4-5 minutes.

6. Remove the pan from the heat and add in the peanut butter, whisking until totally melted.

7. Transfer the mixture to a suitable medium-sized bowl and allow to slightly cool for several minutes, occasionally stirring to prevent skin forming.

8. In the meantime, arrange the pie crusts on a cookie sheet.

9. Add 2 teaspoons of grape jelly to the bottom of each crust, smoothing out a little using the back of a spoon.

10. Evenly divide the cooled pudding between the crusts.

11. Using the back of a spoon spread the pudding to the edges of the crusts.

12. Press kitchen wrap directly onto the top of each pie and chill for 4 hours, or until set.

13. In a bowl, and using a hand held mixer, whip the cream with the powdered sugar until stiff peaks begin to form. Transfer to the fridge until ready to assemble.

14. Whisk the remaining grape jelly with 2 teaspoons of water until silky.

15. Add a dollop of whipped cream to the top of each pie, and with the back of dessert spoon, make a small well in the middle of the cream.

16. Add a small blob of grape jelly into the well and scatter with chopped nuts.

(23) Triple Layered Icebox Cake

Nobody will ever guess you threw together this heavenly chilled dessert in under 10 minutes!

Makes: 12

Cooking Time: 10mins

List of Ingredients:

- 12 chocolate-vanilla ice cream sandwiches
- 1 cup smooth peanut butter
- ½ cup raspberry jelly/jam
- 8 ounces thawed cool whip

MMMMMMMMMMMMMMMMMMMMMMMMMMMMMMMMMMMM

Methods:

1. On a plate or small cookie sheet lined with foil, arrange four of the ice cream sandwiches in a single layer, next to each other.

2. Spread the sandwiches with ½ a cup of smooth peanut butter and then a ¼ cup of jelly/jam.

3. Arrange another 4 ice cream sandwiches over the top. Repeat this layering one more time, making sure the final layer is of ice cream sandwiches.

4. Cover the 'cake' all over with the cool whip and pop in the freezer until ready to slice and serve.

(24) Nutty Nice Cream

Nice cream? That's ice cream with all the nice things added! These include real vanilla, smooth organic peanut butter, and sweet berry jelly.

Makes: 8-10

Cooking Time: 8hours

List of Ingredients:

- ½ cup smooth organic peanut butter
- 1½ cups whole milk
- 1½ cups granulated sugar
- 1½ cups half and half
- ¼ teaspoons kosher salt
- 2 cups heavy whipping cream
- 1½ tablespoons 'real' organic vanilla extract
- 1 cup raspberry jelly

MMMMMMMMMMMMMMMMMMMMMMMMMMMMMMMMMMMM

Methods:

1. Add the peanut butter and milk to a saucepan over low heat. Gently heat, while stirring, until the milk and peanut butter are combined. Take off the heat and allow to cool.

2. Add the sugar, half and half, salt, whipping cream, and vanilla extract. Stir well until combined.

3. Transfer the mixture to an ice cream machine and churn according to the manufacturer instructions.

4. When the ice cream has finished churning find a large freezer-safe container.

5. Spoon ⅓ of the ice cream into the base of the container and top with ⅓ of the raspberry jelly. Repeat this layering twice more.

6. Freeze for 4-5 hours until firm.

(25) Sweet Breakfast Omelet

Sweeten up a regular omelet with peanut butter and grape jelly.

Makes: 1

Cooking Time: 8mins

List of Ingredients:

- 2 medium eggs
- ⅛ teaspoons water
- 1 teaspoon butter
- 3 teaspoons smooth peanut butter
- 2 teaspoons grape jelly

Methods:

1. In bowl, beat the eggs along with the water until combined.

2. In a 7-10" skillet over moderate to high heat, melt the butter. Tilt the skillet to coat the pan and pour in the egg mixture, ensuring that it fills the whole surface of the skillet.

3. Push the cooked egg portions from the edges towards the middle of the pan, so that any uncooked egg can reach the hottest part of the skillet.

4. Continue to cook, while swirling and tilting the skillet, moving the cooked portions around the skillet as necessary.

5. When sufficiently cooked and no uncooked egg remains, transfer the omelet to a plate.

6. Spread with peanut butter and grape jelly.

7. Fold the egg over while the omelet is hot as this will melt the filling.

(26) PB&J Popcorn

Home movie nights just got a whole lot tastier! The family will go crazy for this PB&J coated popcorn.

Makes: 6

Cooking Time: 1hour

List of Ingredients:

- Nonstick cooking spray
- ⅔ cup strawberry jelly
- ⅔ cup smooth peanut butter
- Pinch kosher salt
- 12 cups popcorn (popped)

Methods:

1. Preheat the main oven to 200 degrees F. Cover a cookie sheet with parchment and spritz with nonstick spray.

2. Add the jelly, peanut butter, and salt to a saucepan over moderate heat and bring the mixture to a boil while stirring. Immediately take off the heat.

3. Add the popcorn to a bowl and pour over the hot PB&J mixture a little at a time, while stirring, until the popcorn is evenly coated.

4. Spread the coated popcorn out on the cookie sheet in an even layer and place in the oven.

5. Bake for half an hour, removing every 10 minutes to toss the popcorn.

6. Allow to cool completely before serving.

(27) Sweet and Simple Casserole

Deliciously sweet dessert casserole to share – but only with your best friends!

Makes: 4-6

Cooking Time: 3hours 5mins

List of Ingredients:

- 2 (12 ounce) rolls biscuit dough (cut into quarters)
- ¾ cup smooth peanut butter
- ¾ cup grape jelly

MMMMMMMMMMMMMMMMMMMMMMMMMMMMMMMMMMMMMMMM

Methods:

1. Grease a (6-7 quart) slow cooker.

2. Arrange the dough in the slow cooker.

3. In a medium saucepan, over moderate to high heat, melt the peanut butter while continually stirring, until melted.

4. Drizzle the peanut butter over the top of the dough.

5. In a pan, melt the grape jelly and drizzle over the melted peanut butter.

6. Cover and cook on low for between 1½ -3 hours or until the center is totally set.

(28) Peanut Butter & Grape Jelly Marshmallows

Peanut butter and jelly flavor marshmallow candy is ideal to serve at a kid's party.

Makes: 30 pieces

Cooking Time: 3hours 50mins

List of Ingredients:

- ¾ ounce gelatin
- ½ cup cold water
- 1 cup granulated sugar
- 1⅔ cups grape jelly
- ¼ cup water
- Pinch salt
- Confectioner's sugar
- 6-8 tablespoons smooth peanut butter

MMMMMMMMMMMMMMMMMMMMMMMMMMMMMMMMMMMMM

Methods:

1. In the bowl of a stand mixer, bloom the gelatin along in the cold water, and put to one side for 10 minutes, to rest.

2. In the meantime, in a pan, combine the sugar with the grape jelly and ¼ cup of water. Bring to boil over moderate heat, boiling for 60 seconds.

3. Add the mixture to the gelatin and whip for 10-12 minutes, on high speed, until the mixture has increased in volume and is stiff.

4. Transfer the mixture to a half pan lined with greased kitchen wrap.

5. Place another sheet of greased kitchen wrap on top and gently press into a slab of around 1" thick. Allow to set for 3 hours.

6. Transfer the slab to a chopping board, lightly dusted with confectioner's sugar and cut into 30 equal sized pieces.

7. Toss the marshmallows in confectioner's sugar.

8. Using a double boiler, melt the peanut butter.

9. Dip each piece of marshmallow into the melted peanut butter. You only want a small amount of peanut butter as you don't want to overpower the flavor of the jelly. Set the dipped marshmallows to one side to cool to around room temperature and serve.

(29) Puppy Chow

Your favorite childhood snack just got even tastier with peanut butter and jelly coating. Perfect for girl's night-in or to combat those afternoon munchies.

Makes: 12-14

Cooking Time: 45mins

List of Ingredients:

'Jelly' Chow:

- 1½ cups white candy melts
- 8 cups crispy rice cereal squares
- 1 cup boxed strawberry cake mix

Peanut Butter Chow:

- ⅓ cup smooth organic peanut butter
- 1 cup peanut butter chips
- 1 teaspoon vanilla essence
- 8 cups crispy rice cereal squares
- 1¼ cups confectioner's sugar

MMMMMMMMMMMMMMMMMMMMMMMMMMMMMMMMMMM

Methods:

1. First, make the jelly chow; melt the candy melts according to package directions and stir until silky.

2. Add the cereal to a bowl and pour over the melted candy, stirring gently but thoroughly, until coated.

3. Add the cake mix to a large Ziploc bag and add the candy-coated cereal. Shake well until evenly coated. Transfer to a cookie sheet to completely cool.

4. Next, make the peanut chow; in a bowl, combine the peanut butter, chips, and vanilla essence. Melt together using a microwave and stir until smooth.

5. Add the cereal to a bowl and pour over the melted peanut butter, stirring gently but thoroughly, until coated.

6. Add the confectioner's sugar to a large Ziploc bag and add the peanut butter-coated cereal. Shake well until evenly coated. Transfer to a cookie sheet to completely cool.

7. When both puppy chows are cooled completely, combine in a large serving bowl and enjoy.

(30) Protein-Packed Oatmeal

This scrumptious breakfast is packed full of protein and delicious flavor to give you all the energy you need for a busy day ahead.

Makes: 1-2

Cooking Time: 15mins

List of Ingredients:

- ½ cup almond milk
- 1 teaspoon brown sugar
- ½ cup water
- Pinch sea salt
- ⅓ cup rolled oats
- 1 tablespoon grape jelly
- 2 tablespoons organic crunchy peanut butter

MMMMMMMMMMMMMMMMMMMMMMMMMMMMMMMMMMMMM

Methods:

1. Add the almond milk, brown sugar, and water to a saucepan over moderate heat and bring to a boil.

2. Add the sea salt and rolled oats, reducing the heat to a simmer. Stir occasionally and allow to cook for 5-6 minutes.

3. Take off the heat and allow to sit for 60 seconds before swirling in the jelly and peanut butter.

4. Enjoy.

Chapter II - Drinks

MMMMMMMMMMMMMMMMMMMMMMMMMMMMMMMMMMMM

(31) Peanut Power Shake

Adding a scoop of vanilla protein powder not only adds flavor and texture but also makes this shake a fantastic pre or post-workout snack.

Makes: 1-2

Cooking Time: 5mins

List of Ingredients:

- ¼ cup vanilla flavor protein powder
- 1 cup frozen mixed berries
- 1 cup almond milk
- 1½ tablespoons smooth organic peanut butter
- 2 tablespoons oats

MMMMMMMMMMMMMMMMMMMMMMMMMMMMMMMMMMMM

Methods:

1. Add the protein powder, berries, milk, peanut butter, and oats to a blender and blitz until smooth.

2. Pour into a glass and enjoy.

(32) Coconut Milkshake with Peanut Butter and Raspberry Jelly

Kids and grownups will love this peanut punch served in jelly rimmed glasses.

Makes: 1

Cooking Time: 5mins

List of Ingredients:

- 1 tablespoon raspberry jelly
- 1 cup unsweetened, shredded coconut
- ½ medium banana (frozen)
- 1 cup coconut milk
- 2 tablespoons smooth peanut butter

MMMMMMMMMMMMMMMMMMMMMMMMMMMMMMMMMMMM

Methods:

1. Warm the raspberry jelly in a microwave for 10 seconds until runny. Use a spoon to drizzle the jelly around the inside of a tall glass and set to one side for a moment.

2. Add the coconut, frozen banana, milk, and peanut butter to a blender and blitz until smooth.

3. Slowly and carefully pour into the glass trying not to disturb the jelly swirl.

4. Enjoy straight away.

(33) Peanut Butter, Chocolate, and Jelly-tini

It's party time! Get out the glasses and say cheers to Peanut Butter and Jelly Day with this delicious cocktail.

Makes: 8

Cooking Time: 10mins

List of Ingredients:

- 2 tablespoons strawberry jam (to rim)
- ¼ cup salted peanuts (finely chopped, to rim)
- ½ cup smooth peanut butter
- 4 ounces chocolate liqueur
- 3 ounces vodka
- 3 cups ice

MMMMMMMMMMMMMMMMMMMMMMMMMMMMMMMMMMMMMM

Methods:

1. Spread the jam onto a small plate.

2. Scatter the peanuts into a shallow bowl.

3. Roll each martini glass first in the jam and then in the nuts. Set to one side.

4. Add the peanut butter, followed by the chocolate liqueur, vodka, and ice to a blender and process until combined.

5. Pour the cocktail into the rimmed glasses and serve.

(34) Frappuccino, PB & J-Style

A delicious way to get your caffeine fix!

Makes: 2

Cooking Time: 5mins

List of Ingredients:

- ⅓ cup strong-brewed coffee (cooled)
- 4 tablespoons smooth peanut butter
- 1½ cups whole milk
- 4 tablespoons raspberry jelly
- 1 cup good quality vanilla ice cream
- 2 cups ice

MMMMMMMMMMMMMMMMMMMMMMMMMMMMMMMMMM

Methods:

1. Add the coffee, peanut butter, whole milk, jelly, and ice cream to a blender and blitz until smooth.

2. Add the ice and blitz again until no large ice shards remain.

3. Pour into two glasses and enjoy!

(35) Peanut Butter & Jelly Hot Chocolate with Cream and Mallows

Your little ones will love this hot chocolate, but we are guessing you will too!

Makes: 1

Cooking Time: 8mins

List of Ingredients:

- 1 cup whole milk
- ¼ cup cream
- ½ cup semi-sweet chocolate chips
- 1 tablespoon smooth peanut butter
- ½ tablespoons grape jelly
- Whip cream (to serve)
- Mini marshmallows (to serve)

MMMMMMMMMMMMMMMMMMMMMMMMMMMMMMMMMMMM

Methods:

1. Add the milk and cream to a pan and over moderate heat, bring to simmer.

2. Add the chocolate chips, while occasionally stirring, until melted.

3. Add the peanut butter followed by the jelly and stir until melted.

4. Pour the hot chocolate into mugs.

5. Top with whip cream, and mini marshmallows.

(36) Fully Loaded Milkshake

A super thick and indulgent milkshake choc full of tasty peanut butter, jelly and ice cream.

Makes: 1

Cooking Time: 5mins

List of Ingredients:

- 2 tablespoons smooth organic peanut butter
- 2 tablespoons grape jelly
- 1 cups good-quality vanilla ice cream
- ¼ cup whole milk
- Whip cream
- Glace cherry

MMMMMMMMMMMMMMMMMMMMMMMMMMMMMMMMMMMMMM

Methods:

1. Add the peanut butter, jelly, ice cream, and milk to a blender. Blitz until smooth.

2. Pour into a tall glass and decorate with a dollop of whip cream and a cherry.

3. Enjoy.

(37) PB&J Shooter

Only two ingredients are needed to create a powerful shot with all the flavor of your favorite sandwich.

Makes: 1

Cooking Time: 2mins

List of Ingredients:

- ½ ounce raspberry liqueur
- ½ ounce hazelnut liqueur
- Whip cream

MMMMMMMMMMMMMMMMMMMMMMMMMMMMMMMMMMMM

Methods:

1. Combine both liqueurs in a shot glass and top with a small dollop of whip cream.

2. Down in one!

(38) Oh! So Sweet Smoothie

Now you can enjoy all the flavors of a PB&J sandwich in a glass!

Makes: 2

Cooking Time: 10mins

List of Ingredients:

- 1 medium banana (peeled)
- ½ cup almond milk
- 2 tablespoons smooth peanut butter
- ½ cup frozen strawberries
- ½ cup ice cubes

MMMMMMMMMMMMMMMMMMMMMMMMMMMMMMMMMMMMM

Methods:

1. Add the banana, milk, peanut butter, strawberries and ice to blender, and blitz until silky smooth.

2. Pour the smoothie into 2 glasses and enjoy.

(39) PB&J Party Punch

Kids and grownups will love this peanut punch served in jelly rimmed glasses.

Makes: 4-6

Cooking Time: 10mins

List of Ingredients:

- 4 tablespoons raspberry jelly
- 4 tablespoons peanuts (chopped)
- Ice
- 1¾ cups water
- 1¾ cups evaporated milk
- 3 tablespoons smooth peanut butter
- 2 teaspoons vanilla essence

MMMMMMMMMMMMMMMMMMMMMMMMMMMMMMMMMMMM

Methods:

1. Spread the jelly out onto a shallow dish and the chopped peanuts onto another.

2. Dip the rims of 4 large or 6 small serving glasses first into the jelly and then into the peanuts to coat. Fill with ice and set to one side.

3. Add the water, milk, peanut butter, and vanilla to a blender and blitz until smooth. Pour into the rimmed glasses and serve.

(40) Over 21's PB& J Boozy Bourbon

Definitely one for the grown-ups; enjoy your favorite childhood flavors but fused with bourbon to make a creamy, boozy shake.

Makes: 3-4

Cooking Time: 3mins

List of Ingredients:

- 1 pint strawberry ice cream
- 4 teaspoons strawberry jelly preserves
- ½ cup smooth peanut butter
- ¼ cup milk
- 3 shots bourbon

MMMMMMMMMMMMMMMMMMMMMMMMMMMMMMMMMMMM

Methods:

1. Add the ice cream, jelly preserves, peanut butter, milk and bourbon to a food blender and blitz until silky smooth, 30-40 seconds.

2. Pour and enjoy.

About the Author

A native of Indianapolis, Indiana, Valeria Ray found her passion for cooking while she was studying English Literature at Oakland City University. She decided to try a cooking course with her friends and the experience changed her forever. She enrolled at the Art Institute of Indiana which offered extensive courses in the culinary Arts. Once Ray dipped her toe in the cooking world, she never looked back.

When Valeria graduated, she worked in French restaurants in the Indianapolis area until she became the head chef at one of the 5-star establishments in the area. Valeria's attention to taste and visual detail caught the eye of a local business person who expressed an interest in publishing her recipes. Valeria began her secondary career authoring cookbooks and e-books which she tackled with as much talent and gusto as her first career. Her passion for food leaps off the page of her books which have colourful anecdotes and stunning pictures of dishes she has prepared herself.

Valeria Ray lives in Indianapolis with her husband of 15 years, Tom, her daughter, Isobel and their loveable Golden Retriever, Goldy. Valeria enjoys cooking special dishes in her large, comfortable kitchen where the family gets involved in preparing meals. This successful, dynamic chef is an inspiration to culinary students and novice cooks everywhere.

••••••••••• ● ● ● ● ● ● ● ●•••••••

Author's Afterthoughts

Thank you for Purchasing my book and taking the time to read it from front to back. I am always grateful when a reader chooses my work and I hope you enjoyed it!

With the vast selection available online, I am touched that you chose to be purchasing my work and take valuable time out of your life to read it. My hope is that you feel you made the right decision.

I very much would like to know what you thought of the book. Please take the time to write an honest and informative review on Amazon.com. Your experience and opinions will be of great benefit to me and those readers looking to make an informed choice.

With much thanks,

Valeria Ray

Made in the USA
Las Vegas, NV
16 October 2021

32478647R10069